Burning In The Silence

Of Love, Longing, Loss, and Separation

SARIQUL ALOM BISWAS

Made with ❤ on the BookLeaf Publishing Platform
www.bookleafpub.in
www.bookleafpub.com

Dedication

Dedicated

to

'Teesta'

My Final Retreat

Preface

This collection of poems is a reflection of my heart's journey—a mosaic of emotions, memories, and dreams stitched together with words. Poetry has always been my sanctuary, a place where I can unravel the chaos of life and find meaning in the quiet moments. These poems are my attempt to capture the ineffable: the ache of loss, the warmth of love, the fleeting beauty of a sunset, and the resilience of the human spirit.I began writing these poems during a time of profound change in my life. Some were born in the stillness of early mornings, others in the restless hours of the night. Each poem carries a piece of my story, but I hope they also speak to yours. Poetry, after all, is a mirror—it reflects not only the writer's soul but also the reader's. To me, poetry is not about perfection; it's about honesty. It's about finding the right words to express what often feels impossible to say. In these pages, you'll find raw emotions, unpolished truths, and moments of vulnerability. I invite you to linger in these verses, to let them resonate with your own experiences, and to find solace or joy in their rhythm.

I am deeply grateful to those who have inspired and supported me along the way—my family, friends, and the countless poets, especially Moumita Alam, an emerging writer and poet from West Bengal, whose work has deeply moved me.

And to you, dear reader, thank you for allowing my words to be a part of your world. May these poems remind you that even in the midst of life's chaos, there is beauty to be found.

With love and gratitude
Sariqul Alom Biswas

Acknowledgements

Writing this poetry book has been a journey of the heart, and I am deeply grateful to the many people who have walked alongside me, offering their support, encouragement, and inspiration along the way.

First and foremost, I want to thank my family—my parents, my children, siblings, and loved ones—for their unwavering belief in me. Your love has been my anchor, and your encouragement has given me the courage to share my words with the world.

To my friends and colleagues who have been my sounding board and my cheerleaders, thank you for listening to my endless ramblings about metaphors and meter and for reminding me why poetry matters. Your presence in my life has been a constant source of joy and inspiration.

I am immensely grateful to my publisher, whose keen eye and thoughtful feedback helped shape this collection into what it is today. Your guidance has been invaluable, and I am so thankful for your dedication to this project.

To the poets and writers who came before me, whose work has moved me and taught me the power of language —thank you for lighting the way. Your words have been my teachers, and I am forever indebted to the beauty you've brought into the world.

A special thanks to my friends, Saidur Rahman and Moumita Alam, both of whom are powerful writers. Without their constant support and inspiration, the task would not have been accomplished. Your support means the world to me, and I am honored to share these poems with you. I hope they resonate with your heart as deeply as they do with mine.

Finally, to life itself—the muse behind every word I write. Thank you for the joy, the pain, the love, and the lessons. Without you, there would be no poetry.

With all my gratitude,

1. Love's True Form

Love is like beauty,
For beauty lies
In the eye of the beholder.

Love can be a tool,
A tool to deceive,
Or a truth to believe.

Love is like water,
When held in a vessel,
It takes its shape.

Love is a bomb—
A force of destruction,
Yet a spark for creation.

Love is attachment,
And when it's denied,
Life becomes a hollow hell.

Love is commitment,
An unyielding vow.
Love is passion,
A fire burning now.

Love is compassion,
A tender embrace.
It is timeless,
Beyond time and space.

Love is a retreat,
A sweet return,
To the comfort
of your nest.

Love is eternal,
A light that will stay,
Guiding our hearts
Forever and a day.

2. The other half of my Soul

The day I met you, the world stood still,
A quiet moment, a heart to fill.
I saw in your eyes a spark, a flame,
A mirror of my soul that whispered my name.

Half of me wandered, lost in the night,
Searching for warmth, for love, for light.
Then you appeared, and the pieces aligned,
You were the half I was destined to find.

In your laughter, I hear a song,
A melody that carries me along.
In your touch, a calm so true,
Finally knew, the day I met you.

No longer alone, no longer apart,
You are the rhythm that beats in my heart.
The other half of my soul, complete,
A love like ours, nothing could defeat.

3. A World Within Us

I didn't just want to be your 'Sahir';
I longed to be your 'Imrose' too—
The one who, even without crafting poetry,
Would stay, unwavering, by your side.

One day, I wish to witness your silence—
To wander deep into a bottomless forest as evening falls.
The sky, moonless and bare,
Yet you'll come to know—
The fireflies held a festival of light,
And the evening stars stood as silent witnesses.
That day, in quiet disbelief, we became one.
Promise me—don't leave anyone behind.

Someday, I may roam the world,
And I'll tell you—
I found you in the Nile, in the Sahara,
Among the tangled jungles of the Amazon,
And in the frozen wilds of Siberia.

Honour, pride, sorrow, and memories will endure,
But perhaps, on that distant day,
We'll become someone else,
Living beyond the bounds of this world.

4. Just for You

I longed to be the words in your poem,
To flow like a river, endless and free.
I wished to be a mountain,
Standing tall—just for you.

I wanted to be the verses of poetry,
Spun softly—just for you.
I dreamed of becoming light,
Glowing only for you.
I wished to be the shade of a pine tree,
A quiet refuge—just for you.

I longed to be the moon in your darkest night,
The untimely rain that soothes your soul.
I wished to be the lone star in a moonless sky,
A garland of fireflies, shimmering—just for you.

To keep you warm in the fiercest cold,
I longed to be the sun in your sky—
Just for you.

And when your chest is torn by burning heat,
I wished to come as a single rain—
Just for you.
But perhaps I was selfish.
So, I could be nothing at all.

5. Who am I?

You always saw the best in me,
But now a dimming light you'll see.
It may hurt, darling, it may sting,
Yet I am both shadow and spring.

A blend of good, a touch of wrong,
The truth within me is fierce and strong.
No longer will I hide away;
Both sides of me have come to stay.

One day you'll find—a worldly man,
No heaven-crafted, perfect plan.
But truth prevails; I cannot feign—
This is who I am, joy and pain.

6. Unspoken Chapters

Some stories end without a goodbye.
A silent tear, a question of why.
The echoes linger, soft and still.
A heart, once full, now bending its will.

The pages turn, the ink runs dry,
Yet memories refuse to fly.
A tale unfinished left apart,
A shadow lives within the heart.

But some stories are yet to start,
A spark ignites, a beating heart.
New horizons, skies unknown,
Seeds of wonder freshly sown.

For every door that softly fades,
A window opens, light cascades.
Life's a book, both vast and wide,
With endless tales to script inside.

7. Whisper of the Void

In a world of shadows, where the sun won't dare,
I sit alone on the creaking chair.
A haunted house, its whispers loud,
Yet silence is my only shroud.

The walls breathe tales of despair and dread,
Echoes of footsteps from the long-since dead.
The air, a chill, like a ghost's faint sigh,
The darkness my partner, no stars in the sky.

Pitch black speaks, though words are few,
Its voice a void, yet hauntingly true.
"Fear not the night; it's where truths reside,
In the folds of silence where secrets hide."

I cling to the dark, my solemn muse,
In its endless depths, my thoughts diffuse.
Alone, yet not; its cold embrace
Holds me steady in this forsaken place.

Life in a dark world, a shadowed art,
Where even fear finds its way to the heart.
And on this stair, I'll forever remain,
Bound to the darkness, my constant chain.

8. Love in the Shadows of Despair

In the depths of an ocean of thought,
Where sorrow dwells, a silent voice fades.
Roaming within a world of darkness.
Love is rare in this barren land.
A heart so heavy, I cannot speak.
Sadness befalls me with crushing might,
Consumes my soul, eclipses my light.

All hope I had is crippled,
By a profound and endless darkness.
I am trapped in despair,
Wandering, lost from the path.
Each day unfolds with a subtle hue,
Where emotions fade and dreams drift away.
Beneath the surface, a tempest rages,
A whirlwind of thought fills each page.

Longing for a ray of hope,
Yet engulfed by clouds of despair.

The earth revolves, from dawn to dusk,
Yet I remain—a shattered vessel.
Amidst a stormy night, adrift,
No dock to hold my wandering ship.

No hand to hold, no solace near,
In this labyrinth of sorrow and fear.
Though my soul is tamed, devastated, derailed,
Entangled, gripped by fear—
A glimmer of hope appears on the horizon,
To rise from the ashes and fulfill my purpose.

For every droplet that falls to the ground,
A new river is born.
Though the journey of life may be long,
I will sing my saga as a mournful song.
When the sun finally rises on the horizon,
I will rise from the debris to start anew,
And, in this way, find the beauty of life.

9. Echoes of Forbidden Love

I love you—not to wage a battle.
Perhaps loving is far easier than being loved.
I say "I love you"—not as a battle cry, but as a vow,
A promise to stand by you against a cruel world.

Saying "I love you" may be an act of audacity,
But still, I will say it until my last breath.
Loving you feels like overstepping the boundaries you
set,
Yet the truth remains—I love you.

Once, in our story, there was a pine forest,
The River 'Teesta', and a dream—
A longing to walk side by side,
Through whispering pines or along the riverbanks...
Perhaps it was only a fleeting daydream.

Dreams and promises dwell in the realm of fantasy,
For we are all flesh and blood.
The land of dreams is not meant for mortals like us.

Just as one day, God cast Adam and Eve
out of paradise for disobeying His command.
15

(* Teesta is a major river of Sikim and the northern part
of West Bengal. It originates in Sikim, then passes
through the northern part of West Bengal and finally
enters Bangladesh.)

10. Broken Heart

You promised,
To hold my hand tightly—forever.
Promises made, oaths sworn,
Yet none fulfilled.

Over and over, my heart shatters,
Falling into the same mistake.
Each wound cuts deeper,
A cycle I cannot escape.

Darkness descends,
Winter falls.
Snow blankets the earth—
Cold, silent, endless.

No hope lingers,
No spring will ever bloom again.
No sunlight will pierce the shadows,
Only endless nights remain.

11. When Light Fades Away

I am drowning in a sea of your memories
Knowing very well that the memories neither return
Nor can they be recreated.
The shadow of despair has swallowed me bit by bit.

My heart is burning every day
The fire gripping my soul
My heart is filled with emptiness
My eyes are filled with tears.
Words left me; only tears remain.
I can no longer bear this burden.
My dreams lie shattered

Now I am afraid of the light.
Since the light abandoned me long ago.
So I embrace the darkness
Now darkness is my soulmate.
Every night is my nightmare.
So, daring to dream is my luxury.

Forgetting you is difficult for me.
But if forgetting me is the key to your happiness,
Then forget me.
But I will not forget you.
If leaving me makes you feel more stress-free,
Then let it happen.
But I will still hold you in my heart forever.

12. Echoes of Lost Compass

Once filled with hope and boundless drive,
Never straying, always alive.
Now I drift like a leaf in the wind,
A fate I never thought I'd find.

I never imagined destiny would lead me here,
With no way back, no chance to steer.
Once a man of will, defying all strife,
Now buried in sand, a burden to life.

Once I preached, "Never lose hope,"
Now a captain lost, unable to cope.
No sun upon the distant sea,
No path that leads back home to me.

Once a believer in trust and grace,
Now doubt is all that takes its place.
And so I seek the final breath,
For only truth remains in death.

13. Life and Death

Life and Death, I walk between,
Both my friends, unseen yet keen.
One a spark, fierce and bright,
The other a cloak of peaceful night.

As light and shade, they intertwine,
Guiding steps, both yours and mine.
One offers dreams, the other rest,
Together they shape our very best.

No fear, no fight, just harmony,
Life and Death — my destiny.

14. The Night I Took My Life

The night was a long, reflecting my soul,
A battle within, a story untold.
The whispers of doubt danced in my ear,
Yet somewhere within was a spark, sincere.

I took my life—not to an end,
But to transform, to break and mend.
To gaze in depths where truths unfold,
To sift the ashes, cradle the gold.

The stars stood watch, silent and near,
Witnesses to both courage and fear.
And in that stillness, I found my voice,
To claim my life, to make my choice.

For taking a life can mean to reclaim,
Not an end, but a rekindled flame.
This is not death, but resurrection's art,
A rebirth, a mending of a fractured heart.

A dawn unfolds, where shadows part,
A transformed soul, a brand-new start.
New dreams awaken, vibrant and bright,
To be cherished, nurtured, in the morning light.

15. I'm in COMA

Darling, I'm in a COMA now.
Do you know what COMA is?
A state of prolonged unconsciousness,
Where one can't move their body.

In my case, I can move my parts,
But not my mind or soul.
Unlike in a dream,
Where the soul moves freely,
Here, only my body moves.

My consciousness left
The moment you did.
My body moves without will,
Like a driverless car.

My soul is trapped in stillness,
Disconnected from the world.
I can't taste the foods
You once chose for me.

Now, I am a zombie, roaming in a Zombieland—
A corpse resurrected by witchcraft.

16. A Poem Unfinished

You are not near,
Yet you linger in the hollow of my heart,
A quiet ache, a shadowed part.

You are not near,
Yet you dwell in the silence of my final night,
A whispered echo, a fading light.

You are not near,
Yet you reside in the gray glow of the waning day,
A soft reminder, a muted ray.

You are not near,
Yet you stretch across the vastness of the endless blue,
A boundless thought, forever true.

You are not near,
Yet you breathe in the lines of my unfinished verse,
A silent muse, a blessing and a curse.

You are not near,
Yet you shimmer in the midnight's silver gleam,
A distant star, a fleeting dream.

You are not near,
Yet you rest in the dewy grass beneath my feet,
A tender touch, a memory sweet.

You are not near,
Yet you've become the polar star of my twilight sky,
A constant guide, as time drifts by.

17. If We Meet Again

Once love birds in a soaring flight,
Now two distant souls, divided by light-years,
Residing in different universes.

If we are reborn,
Shall we be strangers,
Or familiar ones?
Will our souls reconnect,
And find their way to be soulmates again?

Is it possible to roam freely once more,
Unbound by obstacles that kept us apart?
Can we feel the same unspoken vibe,
When we meet again, heart to heart?

18. War

To someone,
War is humane,
A necessary evil,
A harbinger of peace.
War is geopolitics,
A game of domination,
A kind of meditation.
War is peace, they say.
But war is business,
Nothing more than that.

But for those who have no voice,
Who cannot choose,
To them,
War is pain,
Destruction and debris,
Homelessness
And mass displacement.

War is an untimely death.
A total extinction,
War is mass destruction
Dehumanization.
An endless cycle of loss and grief.
A deep, insurmountable wound,
And dreams reduced to dust.

19. Smell of Death

How does death smell? Do you know?
Most of you don't, do you?
Is it sweet, like a sickly perfume, or a foul stench?
For them, the smell of death fills their lungs every day.

Death embraces their souls with blood-soaked daggers.
Every street becomes their graveyard,
Every day, a new 'Nakba.'
Did they grow up with war?

And yet, they never become immune to it.
They do not seek compassion,
For compassion cannot resurrect the dead,
The ones who once walked among them.

Those were the people
Who lived to keep memories alive.
On the other side of the universe,
The smell of death is different—
Sweet, not stinky.

Every morning begins with a celebration—
Of death, of joy in counting bodies,
A perfect, grotesque, orgasmic revelry,
Like a hyena feasting on its prey.

20. Retreat to Serenity

Far away from the bustling city
Let's escape to somewhere, untouched—
Where the light of civilisation has yet to intrude
Where the sun glows above by day,
and the moon and stars shimmer at night,
Where a river flows with sparkling waves
and pine forests whisper with their rustling leaves.
Where the birds' chirping can still be heard.

Let's walk along the riverbank one day
beneath the forest canopy.
When we get tired of walking,
We will lie down on the green grass,
And look up at the endless blue sky.
When night falls, we will count the stars,
And when our eyelids grow heavy with exhaustion
We will close our eyes,
And dream together until the sun rises.

I have dreamed of this

Since the moment I conceived you in my heart.
Maybe I didn't live up to expectations,
For I am not as flawless as you once thought.
But this time, I promise to be whole.

21. Teesta: My Final Retreat

I will return again and again
To the banks of the river Teesta
Or to that whispering pine forest,
Drowning in a sea of your memories.

Perhaps, you might encounter me
Strolling on the hillside,
A Spanish guitar in hand—
Or an alms bag slung across my shoulder—
A wandering madman lost in his world.

Perhaps one day you'll notice me.
On the empty stretches of the river Teesta,
Etching meaningless patterns
With broken pebbles in the sand,
Or maybe in a tea estate,
as a worn-out worker.

And then, one day,
You will find me at last—

A lifeless, unclaimed corpse,
Frozen in a silent bed of ice.

www.ingramcontent.com/pod-product-compliance
Lightning Source LLC
La Vergne TN
LVHW050949200726
843508LV00011B/2485